CLASSROOM

Ms. Harris,

Thank you for the difference you make!

[signature]

CLASSROOM

Cradle, Crucible, Crystal Ball

DARBY CHECKETTS

Cornerstone Pro-Dev Press
South Jordan, Utah - USA

Copyright © 2013 by Darby Checketts
All Rights Reserved.

No part of this book may be reproduced without written permission from the publisher or copyright holder, except for a reviewer who may quote brief passages in a book review or other persons who may quote the book with proper authorship credit given. No part of this book may be stored in a retrieval system or transmitted in any form or by any means electronic, mechanical, photocopying, recording, or other without written permission from the publisher or copyright holder. Cover photo: ©iStockphoto.com/darbychecketts.

Cornerstone Pro-Dev Press
Division of Cornerstone Professional Development
PO Box 95961
South Jordan, UT 84095 – USA

Phone: 801-253-0895 or 866-654-0811

Email: info@prep4ed.com

Website: www.Prep4Ed.com

Printed in the USA by *CreateSpace*

Dedication

This book is dedicated to the public school teachers and administrators of the State of Arizona who served me as a boy and to the devoted public school teachers and administrators of the State of Utah with whom I now serve as a substitute teacher.

Acknowledgements

I sincerely thank the many students I have been privileged to teach over the years—the employees of the fine organizations that have been my business clients and the youth of our local school district. When I am in the classroom with you, it becomes the most energizing arena of my life. I recall a recent substitute teacher assignment where my day in the sixth grade ended with the rehearsal of a musical spoof of Shakespeare's play, *Macbeth*. I sat on a stool at the front the classroom and sang along with a roomful of eleven and twelve-year-olds. It was a near-heaven experience to be in that room and listen to those young voices expressing such talent and enthusiasm.

Sharon Barrow Checketts, you are my loving and most trusted companion. You have supported me and joined me in my crusades over the years. Thank you. There are others who indirectly contributed to the insight that made this book possible. I will thank you when we meet again and give you a copy.

Table of Contents

Preface		5
Chapter 1	The Tiny Steward of Glue Bottles	7
Chapter 2	As Smart as You Think You Are	11
Chapter 3	Young Archimedes / Learning	15
Chapter 4	Substitute Teacher: Moment of Panic	23
Chapter 5	Cradle, Crucible, Crystal Ball	31
Chapter 6	Teachers: Noble Profession	36
Chapter 7	Parents: Laying the Foundation	41
Chapter 8	Students: Creating Your World	51
Chapter 9	America: The Education Nation	63
Summary	Blessings / Challenges	66
The Author		73

PREFACE

This is a shorter book than I usually write, but a longer book is not necessarily better. I increasingly appreciate books that just jump right in and get your attention by directly engaging you in the book's real story or message. So, this is my *jump right in* book.

The Book's Message: Perhaps America's top priority is not the economy. It's not healthcare. It's not national security. It's not the national debt. It would appear to be *the effectiveness of the educational processes* that we employ in preparing our children to take over the leadership of our nation. They will be the innovators who drive economic growth, streamline healthcare, protect our environment, and assure our nation's security including its fiscal health and international credibility.

Please Note: The stories and observations in this book are based on my actual classroom experiences while retold with a genuine respect for the privacy of persons. All opinions are those of the author. No other endorsement of these ideas is implied.

Tiny Steward

This little gal was simultaneously the picture of innocence and of self-determination. She had what is increasingly valued as true "grit."

CHAPTER 1
The Tiny Steward of Glue Bottles

At first, she appeared somewhat frail. It was that slender face and those Dickensian eyes...

I recall one of my early assignments teaching 4th grade. Upon returning home at the end of the school day, I told my wife I felt drained. "Those little kids are special, but they can be so needy," I said. "They continuously need reassurance and reminders to stay on task." My day in the 4th grade was an oftentimes joyful day of organized chaos.

About one hour into our afternoon classroom session, I instructed the children to work on an artwork project, which was to illustrate the earth's water cycle. They were to use cotton balls in various shapes and configurations to represent the different types of clouds and to glue these cotton clouds onto their blue construction paper illustrations.

There was soon much creativity in the air...and there were four boys in the corner of the room wrestling. I channeled the wrestling energy into a pretense of doing artwork.

As things settled into a state of *colored-pencil scribbling, mixed with the manipulation of tiny cotton clouds by little hands*, I took a deep breath and thought I would have a moment of peace.

Then, the diminutive girl with that willowy face came forward to explain to me that her regular teacher had given her responsibility for all the Elmer's glue bottles. She was to keep track of these and be sure they were not plugged up and were ultimately returned to the supply cabinet with their caps screwed down. In her hand, she held one of the glue bottles. With a look of distress, she explained that its cap would not tighten and that the opening was clogged with glue. She asked what she should do. I offered to help. She emphatically told me that she alone must do whatever was needed. I offered a paper clip as a tool. She was not impressed and returned to her desk. She took out a pair of scissors. She looked intently at the top of the glue bottle as if she were preparing for brain surgery. She began to poke at the top of the bottle. I walked over to her desk and cautioned her about poking her eye out or cutting her hand. She insisted on persisting. Her glue bottle repair project went on for more than 30 minutes until she triumphantly came forward to declare that the bottle cap was working.

My grandfatherly instincts prompted me to give this dutiful child a genuine hug, but I remembered the guidance in my substitute teacher's handbook. With my hands clasped, I stooped down, smiled at her, and summoned the utmost sincerity to tell her how much I admired her conscientious stewardship over the glue bottles. We talked briefly about what it means to be a "steward."

This little gal was simultaneously the picture of innocence and self-determination. She had what is increasingly valued as true "grit." I could only begin to imagine how much her parents must love her. I realized what a trust had been placed in me to teach and to learn from 4th graders.

Smart Enough

"Yes, Zac, you are smart. You have the right gears in your head and they're turning. You just need to decide in which direction you want those gears to turn and to learn to focus."

CHAPTER 2
As Smart as You Think You Are

That busy boy with the pleasant smile and the sandy-colored hair...I'll call him "Zac" (not his real name). His attention span was about 90 seconds to two minutes. He fidgeted. He wandered. He talked. He was a friendly distraction to others....

My substitute assignment was at a nearby middle school. The day consisted of six 45-minute class periods. I would face over 150 thirteen and fourteen-year-olds before the day was done. What was I thinking?

Thank goodness for the teacher's detailed lesson plans and one educational video that was narrated by a very personable teenager. The class periods went by quickly. Most of the students were on task with the exception of those four or five students in each class who were sufficiently distracted to eventually unglue the concentration of their fellow classmates. Zac took the cake, as they say. He was not disrespectful or mischievous. He just had a dozen other things going on in his mind that competed with studying.

I would remind, cajole, and then firmly admonish Zac to settle down. The effect always lasted for about 90 seconds to two minutes. Near the end of the class period, as the other students had settled into a relatively sane study pattern, I went over to his desk and leaned upon it. I looked him in the eyes with great intensity and asked, "Zac, just how smart do you believe you are, on a scale of 1 to 5, with 5 being the smartest?" He responded immediately, "I'm a two." I quickly and firmly replied, "There's no way you're a two. How do I know? Well it has nothing to do with your appearance. I can't judge how smart a student is by just looking at him or her or even by their physical behaviors. However, I can form some judgments based on how well a student communicates. Zac, you are very articulate, which means you use words well and can express yourself easily. Zac, you are a 4.5 on the smart scale, I'm sure." He paused and in the most thoughtful manner asked, "Do you really think so?" "Yes, Zac, you are smart. You have the right gears in your head and they're turning. You just need to decide in which direction you want those gears to turn and to learn to focus."

I asked Zac to tell me a little something about himself. He described himself as a normal, somewhat happy-go-lucky kid. At home, he is loved and yet his young life is not without its challenges. There are so many factors that affect a child's performance at school. Without walking in each child's shoes, we cannot understand what may be contributing to the particular behaviors we observe in the classroom. Our role as teachers is to be a reliable friend who believes in each child and who also expects him or her to be accountable.

The bell rang. Class was dismissed. Zac said goodbye with what I knew to be a new level of respect and appreciation for me as a teacher. I felt a new appreciation for him.

Later that afternoon as I was teaching my 6th period class, there was a mildly disruptive knock on the open door and I saw Zac standing there in the hallway. The students in the room turned to look. We all saw Zac grinning at me as he held up four and a half fingers and then gave the thumbs-up sign. I smiled at him and returned the thumbs up. The students chuckled and went right back to work. Is it too trite to say that this is what it's all about? This is the reason I honor school teachers. If a teacher makes it through a hectic day in a classroom refilled with teenagers six times and manages to lift just one boy to reconsider himself as smart, it's all worth it.

Young Archimedes

One of the principal ways to lengthen the lever you bring to lifting your own world is to gain more education.

CHAPTER 3
Young Archimedes / Learning as Leverage

All children must climb to the top of a mountain to each find that special staff, which is there to assist with life's journey. The saplings they cut down will be the education they gain. This education will provide the leverage they need to move boulders, to open gates, and to reach their dreams.

I am a great fan of the ancient Greek mathematician, Archimedes. He once said, "Give me a lever long enough and a place to stand and I could lift the world." When he said he could lift the world, did he mean the physical world—wherein his proposition is valid—or was he referring to *his own world*? I think yes, and yes. One of the principal ways to lengthen the lever you bring to lifting your own world is to gain more education. This chapter is a parable. Let's now imagine how young Archimedes came to value his education and to develop such an inquisitive mind.

Young Archimedes Learns – A Parable

Young Archimedes was awakened from a deep sleep by the bright light that suddenly filled his bedroom. In the midst of the light, he thought he saw a childlike fairy or perhaps an angel who softly spoke these words, "My young friend, don't be frightened. Mine is the face of your future. It is bright and full of hope. I have come to give you these instructions. You are now ten years old. Since you were a tiny boy, you have dreamed of climbing the sacred mountain that lies at the end of the beautiful valley you call home. Until now, you have been too young for such an adventure. Your father had planned to carry you or to accompany you up the mountain, but he has grown older and the journey would now be too strenuous for him. You have become strong. You are no longer afraid of the darkness. With me to guide you, you can now make the journey on your own. Tonight I will tell you why this dream of the mountain has been so vivid inside your young mind."

The angel continued, "Midway up the mountain, there is a very young tree, a sapling. It is nearly as old as you are. The sapling is six feet tall and very sturdy. It grows for one purpose alone—to become a staff for you to use on your journey and to show you the way to accomplish the greatest feats of your life. Young man, are you ready to go to the mountain?"

Archimedes inquired, "Must we begin tonight?"

The angel went on, "Not tonight, but tomorrow morning when the sky is first light and the sun is still behind the hilltops. Bring with you bread, cheese, fruit, water, and the small saw that hangs near the door in your father's tool shed. Bring your cloak. Tell no one of your destination, but write a note to your beloved parents to comfort them in your absence.

"Tell your parents that you are in the company of an angel who will protect you and who must lead you to discover your future. Place this golden key on top of your note. They will have never seen one like it before and yet they will know that it is a sign of my power to protect you."

Young Archimedes had never walked so far from his home before. The other end of the valley came closer and closer. He could see the trail that led up the beautiful green mountain, which the people of his village believed to be sacred. The angel had disappeared from his view, but, inside his mind, the angel continued to speak with a soft voice of reassurance that guided his footsteps. Archimedes began his climb.

At times, the path was easy. The birds sang in the trees as sunlight glistened through their branches. Then, suddenly, the way became dark as clouds moved to block the sun. The branches of the trees appeared to gather around him. The path became steeper, rocks were more prevalent, and he found himself climbing hand over foot to keep his balance.

By mid-afternoon as the sun was setting in the west toward his home, he could see the top of the mountain. Now the angel spoke very clearly in his mind's ear and said, "Watch for a sapling that grows at the side of the pathway and leans just slightly across it, as if to stop you in your tracks. A small bird will be sitting in its branches and call your name. As you approach, the bird will fly away. Hold the tree in your hands. Say a prayer of thanksgiving for the added stability it will provide on the remainder of your journey. Take your saw and gently cut it down making sure the cut is straight and clean. Trim all the small branches from the sapling so it is smooth for you to hold."

The angel continued, "When you have finished cutting the tree, sit and rest briefly. As you sit, eat some of the bread, the cheese, and the fruit that you have carried in your knapsack. When you are ready to complete your journey to the mountain peak, walk briskly and whistle as you do. Your new staff will give you confidence as the path becomes steeper. However, assisting you in climbing the mountain is the staff's secondary purpose. Its greater purpose will be revealed as you turn and travel down the mountain on your journey home. You will meet others on your way down who will need your help. Befriend them and do what you can to assist them."

Archimedes continued his climb to the top of the mountain. The climb was both strenuous and exhilarating. On top of the mountain, he could see forever it seemed. He could see in every direction toward mountains and valleys he had never known to exist. His curiosity about the world leaped. He imagined other adventures that awaited him on his life's journey in the years to come.

Archimedes turned back toward the valley that was his home. As he walked, he met others from the village on their way up the mountain. He remembered what the angel had said about the greater purpose of his staff. He became curious to know what she had meant.

At one bend in the trail, a small crowd of people had gathered. They were anxiously shouting and moving about, trying to help a small boy who lay at the side of the path. As Archimedes approached, he could see that the boy's leg was wedged under a medium-size boulder. He asked what had happened.

A woman stepped forward and said, "My boy slid off the path and his leg entered a rabbit's burrow under this rock. The rock settled and we can't move it. Can you use your staff to lift it up so we can pull him out?" Archimedes was eager to help. He placed the staff under the rock and easily tilted it upward. The frightened boy was freed. His leg was unbroken. Just a boy himself, Archimedes had come to save the day. The crowd thanked him and then he went quickly on his way.

As Archimedes re-entered the valley at the foot of the mountain, he came upon an old women working to free her three cows from behind a gate so she could lead them home for milking. The gate was stuck. She saw the boy and beckoned for his help with her cows. Archimedes went to her and said, "Please stand back, I'll pry the gate open with my staff," which he did. The woman raised her arms and looked upward with gratitude.

Soon Archimedes could see his home in the distance. He began to walk more quickly. A small girl came running toward him. She cried out, "Boy, my scarf was caught by the wind. It's hanging up in that tree. Can you reach it?" With his arms stretched to the limit and holding the staff high up in the air, Archimedes pricked the edge of the scarf and gently tugged it from the branches. It fell to the ground. The little girl picked it up, quickly hugged him, and ran happily on her way. What a day this had been for a ten-year-old boy, indeed.

As the summer sun sank behind the hilltops, Archimedes entered the front gate of his home. His parents rushed to greet him. His mother spoke, "Son, we were not worried. We knew you were safe. What did you discover? And, by the way, we've heard stories of a boy who helped many townspeople today. They said he was strong beyond his years. Was it you?"

"Yes, mother and father, I think I am the boy they spoke of. But, I confess that this strength is not my own. It was given to me by an angel. It's in the form of this staff that you see. With it, I can lift heavy things, remove obstacles, pry open gates, and reach high in the sky. I can even use it to scare away the fierce dogs. And, I lean on it when I'm tired. It helped me climb up the mountain and to walk safely down the mountain. Poppa, what is its secret?"

Archimedes father spoke. "My son, it is both a staff and a lever. You will remember that you have used small sticks to pry stones from the ground and chase rats from the chicken coop. Now, you have a larger stick. It is so straight and smooth. Carve your initials upon it. Keep it always. With this staff you could lift the world."

"Thank you, Poppa; I will keep it all of my life."

His father replied, "There is one more thing, dear son. To know all the ways you can use it, you must study and learn each day at the village school where we send you. Your teacher knows of wheels and ropes and pulleys and levers and the fulcrums you use with these, and the many other tools that help grown-ups with their work. One day, you will be the master of these tools and teach others. Perhaps you will lift the world. You will certainly lift *your world* by removing obstacles in your path, by opening gates to opportunity, and by reaching high to achieve lofty goals."

Each Child Must Climb the Mountain

Each child must climb to the top of a mountain to find that special staff, which is there to assist with life's journey. Teachers are the angels who will serve as guides along the way. To climb the mountain is *to finish school*. The climber must keep the goal of reaching the mountain peak in mind and not grow weary from the journey. From the top of the mountain, the child will see a panorama of opportunities never seen before. To summit the mountain will be well worth the effort. The sapling that is cut down represents the education each child gains. This education is the leverage needed to move boulders, to open gates, and to reach for the stars.

Give me a lever long enough and a place to stand and I could lift the world. – Archimedes, 287 BC – 212 BC

Substitute Teacher

After an initial moment of panic, the substitute teacher must quickly assimilate much information, be able to think on her or his feet to improvise where needed, and maintain decorum through positive psychology and without any real authority.

CHAPTER 4
Substitute Teacher: Moment of Panic

In the coming chapters of the book, I will address the "classroom" roles, responsibilities, and opportunities of teachers, parents, students, and American citizens. First, I need to acknowledge substitute teachers. Who are they? In our district, some are young college grads who are staying busy while looking for permanent employment. Many subs are certified school teachers who either want just part-time work or who are retired and can't wean themselves away from their teaching addiction. A goodly number of us are "semi-retired" professionals who hate boredom more than the bubonic plague. I happen to be a "corporate educator" who has spent thousands of days in the classroom providing training for the employees of companies, government agencies, and other institutions, including colleges and universities. I love teaching. I take delight in the eagerness of young children to learn and in the exuberance of teenagers.

The substitute teacher is both taken for granted and greatly appreciated. The average substitute teacher is paid relatively little. Fortunately, most of us don't do it for the money. We appreciate the psychic income we gain from being with children in a learning environment and from the sense that we are providing a needed community service. We are not the "real" teachers and we accept that, but our responsibilities can be significant. There are days when I feel under-utilized as primarily a classroom monitor, projector operator, or test proctor. What I'm doing may be essential, but I simply yearn to do some actual teaching, even for a few minutes during each class period. There are days when I know the teacher I'm subbing for would be very thankful for my competence and for the rapport I am able to create with students.

There are distinct aptitudes that a substitute teacher must possess that are of great value. A sub must be willing to enter where other angels may fear to tread. Subs must assimilate a great deal of information in a matter of 15 to 30 minutes. Subs must be able to think on their feet and to improvise as they read between the lines of the lesson plan that each teacher is supposed to provide. A substitute teacher must be able to maintain decorum in the classroom through positive psychology and without any real authority. Here's the scenario…

It's now winter as I write this. Tomorrow morning, I will arise early, pack my lunch, bundle up, get in my frosty automobile, and drive in the dark to a new school following my Google map. I will arrive at the school, find my way to the office, and hope that the busy person at the front desk is in a cheerful mood. I will sign in; get my badge, the room keys, and a substitute folder with the student roll call sheets.

Then, I make my way to the classroom expecting to find a lesson plan on the teacher's desk and avoid a super-big moment of panic. I have been fortunate to only be left without a lesson plan once. I had to improvise and trust the students to tell me what their routine needed to be (somewhat risky as I'll illustrate in a paragraph soon to follow). Most lesson plans are creative and helpful.

Here comes the moment of "initial panic" that actually turns out to be quite manageable. I begin to read the lesson plan. The following will give you a general idea as to what the lesson plan for a 45-minute class at middle school might be:

- *You will teach periods 1, 3, 4, 5, and 6. You will have B lunch and a prep period. For the MWH-B Lunch Schedule, please see the substitute folder.* (In this case, the details about period two and the prep period were not clear. By the way, "H" stands for Thursday.)
- *For the first 15 minutes, have the students read the "Lost Islands" chapter in their literature textbooks on the shelf at the rear of the room. There are students assigned to pass out the books and student packets. A list of these students is to the left of my desk. The packets are on top of the free-standing file unit behind my desk.*
- *After reading quietly, students should answer the five questions on the side white board. They can work with a partner, if they're quiet. Have them turn in their answers with their names at the top.*
- *Finally, have each student update their "record of work done" in their individual packets and return these before the bell rings.*

The panic is this: the lesson plan is a generally helpful guide to what needs to happen, but sometimes things are not in the places indicated. For instance, the student packets may not be on top of the free-standing file unit, but on the floor next to it. Using a little intuitive skill, I scan the room, re-read the lesson plan, and things begin to come together. The bell rings. Then, a girl comes right up to me and further complicates things. She informs me, "Our teacher told us we don't have to read in the literature books today, if we still have work to do on our "Pilgrim" essays. "Okay" is my simple reply.

A boy at the back of room is swinging his sweatshirt in the air as he chases one of the girls to her seat. Another student walks to his desk at the front of the room, sits down, and asks me in a rather loud voice what my name is. I quickly write it on the whiteboard; turn around and welcome the students to class. I ask for everybody's attention and someone tells me about the two-fingered sign they hold in the air when it's too noisy. As soon as I mention the "Lost Islands" chapter, there is a sudden new rush of activity as a number of students automatically get out of their seats and scurry about gathering and distributing the literature books and student packets.

Eventually, *most* of the students are in their seats and things get *mostly* quiet for the next few minutes as students find the designated chapter in their literature books. Then a miracle occurs.

ESL Miracle, Almost

Seated at the front of the row of desks to my right and next to the window is a very friendly Hispanic boy. (I'll call him Enrique, although it's not his real name.) He chats in Spanish with a couple of boys in the next row. He gives me a wave and smiles politely, but doesn't speak to me. As the students proceed with their reading, he dutifully shuffles his papers and turns the pages of his literature book.

I begin to walk among the desks. I stop next to the young man and compliment him on being friendly and on doing his work. He smiles, shrugs his shoulders, and mutters in broken English, "I not know so much English--cannot read book. Sorry." I am surprised and concerned. I ask him to please wait for just one minute as I gesture with my raised index finger to illustrate. (I was tempted to use a little of my limited Spanish but knew I'd soon be in over my head as he would begin to rapidly chat with me in his native language.)

I go to the front of the room and again call the class to attention. I look at the other boys who were speaking Spanish. I ask, "Would anyone be comfortable sitting up front with Enrique to do some English-Spanish translation for him?" Several hands shoot into the air. I pick one boy who has already shown friendliness toward Enrique. He comes forward to Enrique's desk. I provide a chair for him and, for the next 30 minutes, the two boys work together. They turn pages, shuffle papers, chat in Spanish, and write notes (in Spanish) in response to the learning assignments I have given. I am so proud of myself for accommodating such a fine young man who has obviously come to our country in the recent past and who is struggling to learn English.

The chime signals that class is over. There is the usual hustle-bustle, tripping over backpacks, returning of books and student packets, and the famously noisy chatter of teenagers exiting the classroom. I make sure to thank Enrique's helpful translator as he walks by me on the way out.

Then, I notice some students lingering near the front of the room as Enrique finally walks by. He smiles and says in the most articulate manner with no Spanish accent whatsoever, "Mr. Checketts, thank you very much for helping me with English. It was an excellent class and it was fun to have my friend help me. I now feel very comfortable with English."

The group of students who lingered begin to chuckle. I realize the joke is on me. Nevertheless, I demonstrate my flexibility and my diplomacy as I respond to the students. I say to them, "This is wonderful. I have never seen such an effective ESL program in my entire life. Enrique has learned English in just 30 minutes. It's almost a miracle. Have a great day." I knew I'd been had, but I am proud of my quick thinking in handling the outcome. Such are the hazards and the joys of substitute teaching.

The Joy of Observing

As an important footnote to this chapter, I will tell you what happens after I survive the initial moments of panic and settle into the remainder of my classroom experience. I observe. It is an amazing experience to scan the room and look at each student. It is an amazing experience to walk around each classroom and to notice the plethora of creative things each teacher assembles to make the room a pleasant and illuminating place to learn.

As for the students, some are intent on their work. Others are bored. Some are distracted. The distractions might be a growling stomach, a crumpled paper on the floor, a cell phone, or another student. Some students are neat. Others are disheveled. Some look like engineers in the making. Others are noticeably athletic. Some students are very thoughtful. Others are just mildly rebellious.

There was one female student in one of my high school classes who was simultaneously eating a cupcake, playing a game on her mobile phone, and giving the boy in front of her a back rub. I had a hard time convincing her that each of these things was inappropriate and that she needed to stay on task.

As I purposefully stroll about the classroom, I notice lists of "class rules," lists of students with special assignments, maps, famous quotations, artwork, charts showing scientific principles or math formulas, photographs of outer space or flowery meadows, bottles of hand sanitizer, stacks of folders, books, more books, cupboards full of stationery and artwork supplies, lab equipment of various kinds, charts with the ABC's, coat racks with the most colorful assortments of backpacks, bins full of homework assignments, filing cabinets, the American flag, Stephen Covey "Seven Habits" posters, DVD players and overhead projectors, candy jars, plastic bags full of buttons or pretend coins, computers, and each teacher's special desk—neatly organized or showing evidence of the creative struggle that goes on each day.

What an important and marvelous place the classroom is. Each classroom is a tribute to the creativity of the teacher. Each classroom is full of the richness and the potential of humanity.

Classroom: The 3C's

The classroom experience is a prototype of things to come for our nation socially and economically. I wish every citizen could sit in a classroom to contemplate and extrapolate what success or failure in that classroom might mean for America.

CHAPTER 5
Cradle, Crucible, Crystal Ball

Often, when conceptualizing a book, certain words just pop out, sometime in bunches. Thus, the 3C's of *Classroom* as *Cradle, Crucible,* and *Crystal Ball*.

Classroom

Let's first examine our definition of "classroom." A classroom has traditionally been a gathering place for learning. It is typically a room with places to sit and to write, with various instructional tools and resource materials available to support the "live" instruction of a teacher.

A classroom may also be an informal place of learning such as *around the family dining table in your home* or at a work bench on the job.

In our brave new world, there are *virtual classrooms* where we electronically enter an almost magical chamber containing textual information, scientific data, visual images, music, videos, games, and simulations, with access to tutors via an online chat.

These virtual classrooms will become dominant places of learning as our new millennium progresses. We will be faced with the dilemma of using "high-tech" leverage to enhance learning while not sacrificing the "high touch" experience of mingling and conversing with others while sitting at the feet of a wise and perhaps beloved teacher. Technology will leverage educational efficiency and effectiveness, but we must determine how to not minimize the "affective" and "hands on" dimensions of learning.

Cradle

I can easily recall the image of my wife, Sharon, sitting in the rocking chair in the living room cradling our baby after its inconvenient 2:00 a.m. feeding. We have all experienced the cradling effect, literally or figuratively. I even remember my history teacher discussing the "cradle of civilization." It seems that new things need a place of nurturing. The classrooms of our lives are the cradles of our earliest concepts of the world and our places in it. Many of our most fundamental aptitudes and skills are nurtured in these classrooms.

Even adults need the validation and encouragement that a wise and loving teacher can so aptly provide. As a corporate trainer, when I would walk into a conference room full of employees, I knew that our time together was meant to stimulate new ideas, strengthen commitments, and raise the level of cooperation. When I walk into a 4th grade classroom, I know there are precious things growing there. When I enter a middle school classroom, I know there may be a thirteen-year-old boy whose sense of self-worth is still in its infancy and may need special cradling to help it grow.

Crucible

I remember my chemistry teacher with his mortar and pestle grinding away at various substances to first break these down into smaller granules and perhaps to crush and mix these together with other substances. Sometimes the new mixture would be placed in a crucible and then into an oven where intense heat would initiate the chemical reaction that would produce a new compound. There are the crucibles of our lives. The classroom is a crucible where the ideas of teacher and students come together to be mixed and sometimes ground together. Sometimes there's heat. New insights are forged as learning occurs. A crucible is where we demonstrate the willingness to change and the determination to meet life's challenges.

Crystal Ball

A serious observer sitting in a conventional classroom can imagine the probable future outcomes of the learning that is taking place or not. I have sat and watched students attempting to learn and felt dismay at how ineffective the "uniform" lesson plan seemed to be and how distracted some students were. As if looking into a crystal ball, I could forecast problems for our nation as these students grew up with inadequate knowledge and skills for dealing with the world around them. I have also sat and observed students who were fully engaged with the lesson plan, on task, and energized in ways that gave me great hope for our future.

I truly believe that the classroom experience is a prototype of things to come for our nation socially and economically. I wish every citizen could sit in a classroom to contemplate and extrapolate what success or failure in that classroom might mean for America.

As we would observe the students, we might ask ourselves: will the distracted student become withdrawn, unemployable, and dependent? Will the energized student become a highly productive adult who enriches life for others? We must all ask: "What will be the outcomes of each classroom experience that will affect us as families, neighbors, and fellow citizens—directly or indirectly?"

Dedicated Teachers

The teachers I meet are amazing. Their dedication is evident. They work tirelessly. They give back more for their salaries received than perhaps any other single group of American professionals.

CHAPTER 6
Teachers: Noble Profession

Our Teacher's Gone

I remember when I first came to love someone other than my own family members. She was "Mrs. D." That's what we sometimes called her. She was my third grade teacher and the one who helped me learn to love books and to write coherently. She was a wonderful teacher and I believe she loved me as her pupil. Then, one morning, she wasn't there at the head of the classroom. Our principal stood there with a very sad look on his face. As my fellow students came into the room and sat down, our principal wiped a tear from his eye and then told us that our dear teacher had died. A roomful of children instantly burst into tears. Some put their heads down on their desks and sobbed. Others asked "why, oh why" in disbelief. I think I just stared at the principal with tears streaming down my cheeks.

Our principal explained that our dear teacher had stayed after school the previous afternoon to clean up our classroom. She had mopped the floor and, as she scurried about, she slipped on the wet floor and struck her head on the corner of her desk. The blow killed her almost immediately. She was gone.

I asked myself over and over, "How can a boy's favorite teacher die? Why did this happen? What will we do?" My love for teachers instantly grew. I knew why I loved Mrs. D. I knew it very deeply. It was because she loved us and showed it every day by the extra things she would do. She had lost her life while preparing her classroom to be shiny and clean for the children she loved.

Who Do You Owe?

I remember attending a seminar where the presenter made this bold statement: "Many of those who struggle most with life spend their time convincing themselves that the world owes them something. They tell themselves: the government owes me…my wife or husband owes me…my children owe me…God owes me. And so it goes. These individuals paint pictures of themselves as the victims of ungrateful others who do not understand their needs or their value."

The seminar presenter went on to challenge us to turn the tables and consider *who we owe* and that this would be one key to a far more positive attitude about life. He started by asking, "What do you owe to the teacher who patiently and lovingly labored with you that you might learn to read? What has that skill been worth to you in your life? If you had to write that teacher a check for her (or his) contribution, would it be for $50, $500, or perhaps $50,000, or far more? Can you ever repay her? No. And she would not want you to. She gave her time to you out of love and her professional commitment as a teacher. She would only expect that you value and use the great skill she helped you to acquire—that you would read often and enjoy what you learn as you do.

My own sister, Paige, has been a dedicated school teacher for many years. She tells me of the challenges faced by many of the children in her classrooms—of their difficult family situations and the negative impacts on their sense of self-worth that she has to help them overcome as their teacher. We all know many stories of teachers who were and are the rescuers of children whose parents are struggling at life and failing to provide what their children need whether it is security, guidance, or love. I know my sister is one of these rescuers.

Where parents are doing their best and succeeding in many ways, teachers still see things about the children in their classrooms that others miss. They augment the great good that loving parents and guardians do. They have unique opportunities to observe children in a learning environment where their special interests in science, math, literature, sports, the arts, or the applications of technology are revealed. No influence can replace that of loving parents and yet children benefit greatly from a mentor who can speak clearly to them of their potential in ways that parents sometimes do not.

Sharon and I recently watched the classic movie, "Anna and the King of Siam" starring Irene Dunn and Rex Harrison. The king has a son who is the prince and heir to his throne. He hopes that his son will be worthy of the kingship and perhaps be a better steward of the kingdom than his father has been. The movie has a very emotional ending where the king is dying and reflecting on who he owes. Anna comes to his side. The king looks admiringly at her and tries to adequately express his gratitude. His final words are to this effect: "If children are to become better than their parents, it is because of you as their teacher."

While I am a good person who has had a good life, I still hope that my own children will be even more successful and happy than I have been. However, I can't teach them to be what I have not become. I can teach them all that I have learned, but they must also learn from others to expand their horizons. Their school teachers have played key roles as the *multipliers of their talents and skills* so that they might each reach the potential that is uniquely theirs.

I can recall some of my children's school teachers by name. They were powerful and loving friends to our children. Some were as drill sergeants, necessarily so. Some were as sculptors. Some were philosophers. Some were beacons on a hill. All of these teachers expected my children to expect more of themselves and to enrich their understanding of the world around them that they might grow up to make a difference, which they have. I thank God for dedicated school teachers.

My eldest daughter, Natalie, has just graduated from the University of Utah with her Master's Degree in Education. I asked her specifically about her *purpose* and her *passion* as a new teacher. Here is her reply: "My *purpose* in becoming a teacher is to help young people believe in themselves. I see myself as a guide through the fascinating worlds of language, literature, and the life sciences. I encourage students to discover what makes our world such a beautiful and interesting place. My *passion* for teaching grows each time I read something one of them writes that connects their own life experience to a larger social, scientific, or artistic issue."

Loving Parents

Beyond the grave, we only get to keep what's in our brains and in our hearts--not what's in our pockets or purses. As our children succeed in school we help to "fill up their brains." As we demonstrate love, we help to "fill up their hearts."

CHAPTER 7
Parents: Laying the Foundation

I'm a dad. I'm a grandpa. I am also a neighbor, an American citizen, and a man of faith. Professionally, I am a business consultant, trainer, and author. I have also been a Human Resources representative, a manufacturer's sales representative, a work group supervisor, a quality assurance manager, and a company vice president. And, now I am a part-time substitute teacher. It is a humbling responsibility.

All the above roles and responsibilities come and go, except for those of father and grandfather. These are the only roles from which I cannot resign—wherein I am irreplaceable. My genetic ties to my children and grandchildren make it so. The legacy of my time upon this earth will be measured more by how I fulfill these roles than by any of the others. No other success can possibly compare to the contribution I can make as a father and grandfather to benefit our extended family members and the larger society.

The immensely important role of father is one for which I did not receive any formal training. Yes, my upbringing as a youth set a pattern for the kind of father I would become, but I was never expected to go to school to become a dad. No one ever screened me for the job. My contract is not written upon paper. My compensation is not tangible. It is the only role that has permanent consequences. In all the other jobs of my life, I could make excuses for failure and expect the opportunity for a do-over to make things right. As a father, the results of my commitment and skill are permanently written in the lives of my seven children.

My children are now grown. They have their lives to lead. I am proud to say that they have developed an attitude of "ownership," which is to take responsibility for their own lives; to develop the self-reliance to make their own ways in the world successfully and happily. They accept the fact of their free agency to choose and to do for themselves and their families as I did. While they know I had a significant impact on their development, they don't blame me for their struggles or give me undue credit for their successes. For this, I am most thankful. At the same time, not a day goes by that I don't mentally review all seven children by their names and ask myself, "Are they each doing okay? Is there something more I can do to support them?"

Perhaps the best way to examine my effectiveness as a father can be found in the idea of "foundation building." My children have endured their struggles and built their successes upon a foundation that was laid in our family home. I know there were stones that went missing or that were laid more hurriedly than others. I know those stones that were of the utmost importance and

I took extra care as I placed these stones in our family foundation. These stones would help my children to feel secure and to each build their sense of self-worth.

No Perfect Parents

If you were to go in search of the perfect parents, you would fail. There are none. Every parent experiences both joy and heartache. Every parent knows of things that were overlooked or could have been done more conscientiously, and of things that should have been left undone. We would expect that every parent has feelings of joy when a child succeeds and is happy. We would hope that every parent's heart skips a beat when a child stumbles or fails. We ask ourselves, "Was it something I did or did not do?" The answer is that it might have been, but that's in the past. I believe most of us parents do the best we know how as we juggle our parenting responsibilities with everything else that's going on in our lives. As there are no perfect parents, we must all be thankful for the good that we did for our children and for the good that our parents did for us.

So, for whom am I writing this reflective chapter? Perhaps it is not for those of us whose children are grown (and yet many of us now have grandchildren who learn from us and who benefit from our loving concern). I am primarily writing for those parents whose children are now in elementary, middle school, high school, and preparing for college. My reason for including this chapter in the book is to offer some suggestions you might consider that will help you to prepare your children for success in school. You want them to have as firm a foundation as possible so that the power of education will be effective in their lives. I am writing as the father of seven, grandfather of thirty-three, and as one who has spent thousands of days in the classroom with adults, children, and youth.

Many individuals believe that all we can take with us beyond the grave is our knowledge, character, and the value of important relationships. In other words, we get to keep what's in our brains and in our hearts—not what's in our pockets or purses. As our children succeed in school, we will have helped to *fill up their brains* with useful information and skills. As we demonstrate love for our children, we help to *fill up their hearts*.

To Fill Up Their Hearts

Let's start with their hearts. Matters of the heart are tender things. It has been said that we make life's decisions with our hearts and then justify those decisions with our brains. We are more creatures of the heart than we would sometimes admit. When choosing life's truest companions, are we not most concerned about what's in their hearts? When choosing an accountant or surgeon, we may be more concerned about what's in their brains, but even in these cases, it is good to know what is in the heart of your accountant and your surgeon. What can we do to help fill the hearts of our children?

Children need to feel *secure, loved,* and *valued*. There may be a longer list of what they need, but feeling secure, loved, and valued goes a long way. There are many books written about the principles of effective parenting. And, principles of faith establish the moral basis for how we treat our precious children. May I suggest that each week you review your relationship with your children by asking yourself these questions: (a) Do they feel secure and unafraid? (b) Have I shown my love outwardly to them by word and deed? (c) Do they know that I value who they are—that I see their potential as I help them to believe in themselves? And, have I taken the time to enjoy what is important to them and to be there for them as they solve their problems and pursue their goals?

When children's hearts are not full, they do not learn well. When they feel insecure, unloved, or undervalued, their school teachers will carry an extra burden in helping them to see their potential. Parents must constantly strive to send their children to school with their hearts full. I believe this: *what wins the heart will rule the mind.*

To Fill Up Their Brains

To conclude, please allow me to share a number of practical things that my wife and I have learned from our child-rearing experiences and from having coached parents in our community about how to help prepare their children to succeed in school. Pick 3 to 5 of these to work on and move your family to the next level of learning.

1. **Dine Together.** Have dinner together whenever possible. It is amazing how much children learn during mealtime conversations and interactions. They learn to be respectful by practicing table manners (please pass the potatoes). They discover new words and how to carry on a conversation as they share in the family's concerns, happy stories, and good humor. They can recognize the value of good nutrition. They learn about the current activities of other family members and witness the enactment of traditions that grow out of their own family history. And, that initial blessing on the food teaches children to appreciate the bounties of life and the efforts of those who work hard to provide for the family. There's so much to learn at dinnertime. Who would want to miss it?

2. **Study Together.** Designate a time each school night as "study time" for children and for parents. Turn off the TV

and cell phones. After study time, enjoy a favorite TV program and some popcorn, nachos, or brownies.
3. **Read Together.** Read with your children and let them see you reading! Teach them to *ponder* upon what they read to gain the deeper spiritual insight that is often there. It's a powerful word: "ponder." Look it up in the dictionary. By the way, it is generally true that up to and through third grade children *learn to read* and thereafter they *read to learn*. How important is that? How important are grades K, 1, 2, and 3?
4. **Share Learning.** From time to time, when you're all together, have a "learning sharing" time. As parents, lead the way by sharing something you learned that day. Invite your children to do the same. This could be in the family van as you travel along or as part of your special "home evening" activity.
5. **Show Interest.** When your children come home from school, don't put them right to work. Sit down with them and take time to be interested in the fun and social side of school as well as the academics. One dad changed the whole dynamic of his son's school experience by asking, "Did you have any fun at school today?" He had previously asked, "Did you learn anything today?" This had the effect of putting his son on the spot instead of helping his son discover that going to school to learn is also an adventure to be enjoyed.
6. **Befriend Teachers.** Be sure you become well acquainted with your children's teachers, counselors, and school administrators. They are the experts on school activities and student academic performance. You are the expert on your child. The teacher-parent partnership is invaluable.

7. **Develop Your Skills.** As your children pursue their schoolwork, let them know you are taking a language skill or cooking class or some other program of personal and professional development at the local community college or online using the computer and the Internet.
8. **Love Libraries.** Create a family library even if it's just one shelf in the corner of the living room. Put a sign on the wall that says "Our Family Library." Go to the public library together. Visit your neighborhood bookstore to buy a favorite book. Even if you have an iPad or a Kindle-type book reader, collect and read some favorite books in hardcover and paperback formats. Such books give a sense of history and of the excellent work that authors do. These are tangible evidence of what you have studied and learned that you love. *It is exciting to hold a computer notepad. It is a joy to hold an actual copy of a favorite book.*
9. **Tour Colleges.** When your children turn eight, take them on a tour of a nearby college campus to admire the buildings and landscape. Let them begin to envision themselves walking across that campus as they undertake their college educations. Revisit the campus and other campuses periodically. Talk about college as a natural step in their lives as contrasted with something optional they might do or not. Affirm the idea of college life as you would the ideas of fulfilling a missionary calling, defending our country, or getting married and raising children.
10. **Connect Learning.** Help your children make everyday connections with the principles of science and math. Shopping is about math. Changing a flat tire is about physics. Cooking is about chemistry, etc.

11. **Explore Careers.** Expose your children to various career options and help them recognize the educational requirements of these careers. The Boy Scouts, Girl Scouts, Boys and Girls Clubs, and other such youth programs provide excellent ways to expose children to potential fields of interest. Comment to your children on the valuable things that nurses, carpenters, software engineers, chefs, business operators, teachers, chemists, botanists, artists, and others do for society and how education helps each of them to qualify for the work they love and to succeed at it.
12. **Enjoy Mentors.** Encourage your children to find mentors to inspire and assist them. There are many qualified individuals who will gladly volunteer to work with your children. Ask them. There are professional tutoring programs that will be among the most important investments you will ever make.

By doing these things, you will help to create a "Culture of Learning" in your home that will prepare your children to overcome obstacles, to stay the course, and to experience the joy of learning. Their hearts will be full of love and their brains will be full of understanding. And, most importantly, they will know that their parents rejoice *and* their Creator finds glory in their intelligence. This intelligence allows them to experience life more fully and to expand their capabilities for serving others. The more they know, the more they can do to make a difference.

Special Footnote: It is also very important that, before we send our kids to school, we *fill up their tummies* with nutritious food. There are correlations among these: a child's state of mind, level of energy, ability to stay on task…and whether a child had breakfast or not. If it is somehow a challenge to provide your children with an adequate breakfast, there are so many who would assist you. Let them. The blessings will be reciprocal.

Creative Students

Imagine that when you were a child, a wise person came to you holding an artist's canvas and palette and asked you to paint the picture of your future. This is the picture you will live to fulfill. First you set the goal and then you see.

CHAPTER 8
Students: Creating Your World

To gain an education is to undertake "The Art of Creation." Imagine that in your childhood some very wise person who could foresee your future potential came to you holding an artist's canvas and palette. This special friend then said to you, "Here, take these artist tools. I invite you to paint the picture of your future. Once you do, you will grow up and *live into* that very picture. If there is no picture, your footsteps through life will be unsure. You will wander. With a clear picture of your future, you will live out your days in the fulfillment of that vision. Do not sell yourself short. Close your eyes now and dream. See yourself as an adult. Who will you be? What will you do with your time that will be enjoyable and challenging that will make a difference for others? Where will you live? Where will you travel? With whom will you spend your life? Paint the picture."

Over the years, I have delivered many professional development workshops on the topic: "Balancing Your Priorities for a Lifetime of Achievement." The following is some of what I teach.

Note: If you are a very young person reading this book, please invite your parents to read this chapter with you so they can help you to apply the important concepts that are here.

As you paint the picture of your life, you will do it by setting goals. You will also prioritize these goals to determine which goals are most important so that you can allocate enough time and effort to their accomplishment. Let me illustrate the importance of goals in this way. Suppose that I ask you to stand beside me as I hand you a small basketball. Then, I ask you to show me how good you are at throwing the ball. You look around the room a bit puzzled and ask me, "Where should I throw it?" I reply, "Just anywhere you'd like to show me how well you throw." Then you just toss the ball. I'm not impressed and you are even more puzzled. My eyes light up and I say, "Would you like a waste basket to throw it in sort of like throwing it through the hoop at a basketball court." You are relieved. I get a waste basket from the other room. You throw the ball directly into it and shriek with excitement as you tell me, "See, I told you I could throw the ball." The difference was that you finally had a goal, somewhere to throw the ball—somewhere to focus your energies.

Let's talk about career goals, in other words, the jobs you would like to have in the future to help you buy the things you want, live where you want, provide for those you love, and to do good. Such a goal needs to be identified early in your life to help motivate you to stay the course in finishing school and in working hard to prepare yourself for the jobs you prefer to have. Let me illustrate the difference between two students. The first student finishes high school and has no idea what he wants to be when he grows up. He gets admitted to college and signs up for "General Education." Do you know where he is going to go on the first day at college right after he checks in with the front office? He's going to the Student

Center to see who's there to hang out with until classes start, and to get a snack.

Let's talk about a second student. She happens to have been my daughter, Denise. Denise was a high-energy, gregarious young person. Actually, she still is. In high school, she enjoyed hanging out with her friends. She eventually found a very special boyfriend who we (her parents) also liked very much. One day, in her junior year, she "blew our minds." That night, just before dinner, she insisted that we sit down at the table and listen while she told us how much she loved her new Human Anatomy class. She took my arm and laid it out in front of me as she proceeded to describe all the marvelous components of my arm that made it so useful and so valuable to me. She pointed out where the nerves and veins are and how the bones and muscles are attached. She proceeded to tell me about the *extensor digitorum muscle*, the *abductor pollicis longus muscle*, the *extensor carpi radialis brevis tendon*, and other tendons that connect everything to something so that my arm works properly. She could scarcely catch her breath as she exuded enthusiasm for the marvels of the human body.

A couple of months later, Denise burst through our bedroom door one morning as we were just getting up and proclaimed, "Mom, Dad, I know what I'm going to be. I am going to be a nurse and nothing will stop me." We believed her. We were thrilled with the clarity of her vision. She had painted a mental picture of herself in a nurse's uniform inside a hospital assisting doctors and patients. We knew she would "live right into that picture," and she did.

Now where do you think this second student, Denise, went on her first day at college? Did she rush to the Student Center cafeteria to get a snack? No. She could hardly wait to get to the

Nursing Department at the University and to meet the professors who would be teaching her classes.

First you set the goal and then you see. If you do not see BIG, you will not see enough. In other words, the first student I mentioned earlier had no career goal and he could not see the value in the college courses he was about to attend. As obstacles would come along, he would most likely procrastinate his studies and one day find an excuse to drop out of school. On the other hand, once Denise could see that picture of herself in a nurse's uniform, there was nothing that could stop her. The future would not be right if she did not get her hands on that uniform, get hired by a fine hospital, and have the amazing opportunity to nurse people back to health and to even save their lives. *First you set the goal and then you see.* That first student might think to himself: "I can't afford to go to school" or "It's too hard" and then give up. The student who can visualize herself in a nurse's uniform dives in to cruise the Internet looking for nursing programs and for scholarships. She gets a part-time job to earn and save money for college. She studies.

You must see yourself as young Archimedes in Chapter 3. You will come to understand the importance of getting your hands on that lever that will help you to lift boulders out of the way, to open gates for others, and to reach as high as the sky to achieve amazing goals that are about your potential to make life an adventure and to make a difference for others. Here are some of the elements of a *Goal Achieving* process to help you get going, to visualize your future career, and to commit to getting the education you will need.

Here are five steps to help you paint that amazing picture of your future:
1. **Find Your Passion**. Ask yourself: "What are the sources of my physical, mental, and spiritual energy? What do I do especially well? What do I want out of life? What can I imagine myself doing that will be meaningful and exciting?"
2. **Establish Your Purpose.** Ask yourself: "What is it, specifically, that I intend to change, to improve, to achieve, or to contribute that will make the world a better place?"
3. **Set Your Goals.** Begin with what I call your "150 List" that is described in the paragraphs below. This list will be the "Field of Dreams" from which you choose specific goals. For instance, if you'd like to play a particular musical instrument, this might prompt you to one day set a goal to study music at the university and to become a professional musician. If you love building things with your hands and one of the items on your 150 List is to "build a canoe," you might one day choose to study engineering or to pursue one of the various construction trades as your career goal…or you might study business so you can start your own construction company.
4. **Make Plans to Turn Your Goals into Reality.** Answer these four questions:
    a. What must I personally give to get what I want?
    b. What obstacles must I overcome?
    c. What specific steps must be taken?
    d. What resources will I need to assist me?
5. **Envision Your Success.** Affirm the future. Look for role models—other people who do well what it is you hope to do one day. These people can become your mentors. Read books and online articles on the subjects that interest you. Take

relevant photographs, save these on your mobile phone, and post photocopies on your bedroom wall. When you go to bed at night, tell yourself to dream about a concert in which you will perform. Imagine yourself rowing down a river in that canoe you will build.

The 150 List

Now, let's turn to that "150 List" or *Field of Dreams*. Here's how I came to know of such a powerful concept. It was once my great privilege to interview a very accomplished man to ask him the secret of his success. He told me this story. When he was a high school student, he approached one of the coaches at the college he planned to attend to ask the coach what he could do to be prepared. The coach told him to write down a list of 150 things he would like to do with his life. The young man thought this was a huge number, but, as he was just 17 years old and could live to be 92 years old, he realized this would give him 75 years to accomplish 150 things, which is just two per year. The young man set out to create the list, but he soon became frustrated. His initial list seemed uncreative. It included: finish college, get married, get a good job, get a cool car, take my wife on a trip to Europe, buy a nice house, have some kids, and whatever else came along. He was stumped. He called the coach. The coach was disappointed and told him to not call again until he had finished his 150 List.

The young man turned his frustration into a renewed determination to succeed. He began to search through magazines, library books, and television programs to get ideas for creative hobbies, places to travel, books to read, interesting careers, and for powerful ideas that would help to make the world a better place. He asked neighbors and relatives where they had traveled, what their hobbies were, what books they read, and why they chose their particular careers. It took two months, but the young man had his list. As I was interviewing him at his middle-age, he reported to me that his 150 List was nearly two-thirds finished. He said that the secret to his success is that he always has dreams ready to inspire his future vision of life. One by one, the dreams become his goals and then he makes plans to turn these goals into reality. This idea of a "150 List" has blessed my life and the lives of many others with whom I have shared it.

When I created the original version of my 150 list, I dreamed of climbing several important mountains. One of these was Mount Kilimanjaro in Africa. Little did I realize the important, though indirect, effect that "Kilimanjaro" would have on my life. One day, some years later, I was teaching a seminar in London. In the second row of my classroom, there was an African businessman who was very intent upon my teachings. At the end of the day, he came to the front of the room and said, "Mr. Checketts, I like your teachings and I want you to come to my country to teach my people." I asked where he lived and worked. He replied that his business was located in Lagos, Nigeria. At the time, Nigeria was controlled by a military dictatorship. My first thoughts were of the potential dangers. Then, as I was about to excuse myself from a trip to Lagos, the image of majestic Kilimanjaro popped into my mind. Suddenly, my future vision allowed for the possibility of a Nigerian adventure. I asked my new friend, "How far is Lagos from Kilimanjaro?" His answer: "Much closer than Utah where you live now."

To make a long story short, I have traveled multiple times to West Africa where I have had the greatest adventures of my life and where I have formed friendships that have been uniquely powerful over the years. While I have climbed many other mountains, I have yet to climb Kilimanjaro. However, my eldest son, Vance, became inspired to climb in my place. What is most important is that the word "Kilimanjaro" on my 150 List opened-up opportunities that I could never have foreseen or have otherwise allowed myself to consider.

You create your world by how you think and speak about it. If you speak of college as "something that's impossible," you will naturally become discouraged. If you think of college as a burdensome duty, you will become disillusioned by the first boring lecture you hear. Conversely, if you think of college as the gateway to foreign lands, or as the pathway to saving lives, or as the road you must travel to give that concert, or as the journey you must take to become an engineer and the builder of great things, then college will become a time of preparation and discovery. Begin your 150 List now. Perhaps you might be interested to see some of the items on my 150 List.

Selections from Darby's 150 List

- Learn to play the banjo. (I bought one last year, took lessons to get started, and I practice regularly.)
- Learn Spanish. (I am taking computer-based lessons, but need a more consistent schedule.)
- Experience the ocean more often. (I am fascinated by it. I look forward to getting more sand beneath my toes.)
- Perform humanitarian missionary service with Sharon. (Already underway.)
- Take lessons from a master chef in an Italian village. (Looking forward to it.)
- Teach a course at a college or university. (Have done much training for university and college clients.)

- Help someone else learn to read. (My substitute teaching experiences include some wonderful "reading moments" with children of various ages.)
- Travel to all seven continents. (Have been to five including 27 countries; two continents to go.)
- Donate books to children in West Africa. (Done.)
- Take up the sport of fencing. (Recently deleted from my current list. Took up the banjo instead.)
- Address poverty by making regular donations to LDS Humanitarian Aid and Habitat for Humanity. (Ongoing monthly for years.)
- Write useful books that get published, non-fiction and fiction as well. (This is my 14th book.)
- Stay physically fit so I can run, hike, bike, snow shoe, and climb mountains with my wife, children, and grandchildren. (Doing regularly.)

I started my 150 List at mid-life. It has over 100 items. About 70 have been accomplished. My college education was the leverage that allowed me to create the career that has made most of these things possible. *First you set the goal and then you see.* Though my mother never attended college and my father never finished, I decided I needed to set the example for my three brothers and four sisters. I received two scholarships. While in college, I worked part-time 20-30 hours per week. My freshman year, I was bored and wanted to drop out. I met and married Sharon while at college. With parental promptings, we both renewed the commitment to our educational goals. I persevered and graduated with honors. Sharon was pregnant with our second child when she graduated. All seven of our children graduated from college. Several have advanced degrees.

Paint the picture of your future now and set the goal to complete your education. Be prepared. Many things will get in your way as a young student. Here's a partial list:
- boredom,
- too little sleep the night before the big test,
- hunger pains and a craving for cupcakes,
- electronic gadgets with video games and social media,
- the girl or boy who sits in the desk next to yours,
- too many hall passes,
- the occasional grumpy teacher,
- a scary-thick textbook,
- the dread of homework, etc.

Don't let these represent smudges on that picture of your future that you are painting. **Stay on task!** Let me conclude with my 70-15-15 rule. It has been my experience as a substitute teacher that, in nearly every class (but not all), about 70% of the students manage to stay mostly "on task" (OT) while 15% are mildly distracted (MD) and another 15% are seriously distracted (SD). It's up to you to determine where you fit with the 70-15-15 rule. Are you OT, MD, or SD? Be aware and be in control.

As most of us grow older, the habits of our youth are still manifest. There are many adults in the world who spend every day mildly or seriously distracted with a wide range of undesirable consequences. VERY IMPORTANT: Develop the maturity to say NO to *the less important things you may want now* that are often the things that distract you from the task at hand and from your goals, so that you can have *the more important things you will want later in life*. This is a tough lesson to learn when you're just 14 or 17, but you can do it and establish yourself as an extraordinary person.

And, one last note about going to college to study *something meaningful for you* and, at the same time, *something of practical value to others*. If you really, really want to be an actor, go for it, but realize that an actor's average annual pay in the USA is about $23,000 per year. You'll spend most of your career as an "extra" in "B" movies. You might be better off to get an Engineering degree so you can earn a good living while you passionately participate in "community theatre" as a meaningful hobby on the side. With your Engineering degree, you could become an animator for Pixar or you might choose to build bridges that help others to cross rivers for many years to come. The future is yours to create. *First you set the goal and then you see.*

In the end, *choose a career you can learn to love* for you will spend more hours in this pursuit than in any other. Your choice will affect the level of joy you derive from the other arenas of your life: family, church, community, and the cultivation of your own talents and hobbies. The necessity of providing a livelihood for yourself and your family means that "pay" is important. Choose to do something that has practical value for others. However, balance "pay" with "passion" for, if you love what you do, you will do it especially well and the monetary rewards will eventually come. If you would be a teacher, let nothing stop you. If you would be a law enforcement officer to keep our communities safe, we need you. If you would be a violinist, perfect your talent and uplift us. Do what you love so you can love what you do. Explore the exciting career options that will help you to meet multiple objectives, which will assure a balance in life and lasting success. *First you set the goal and then you see.*

Education Nation

Eventually, we will all be living in the future world that today's school children will create. There is much at stake for us all. NBC News has challenged us to be the Education Nation.

CHAPTER 9
Americans: The Education Nation

I remember years ago when I was learning to use word processing software, I became aware of the concept of WYSIWYG (pronounced wiz-ee-wig), which stands for "What You See Is What You Get." This means that, when using an electronic editor, what you see on the computer screen looks like what you will see in the actual document when you print it. I believe there is a close analogy here with our educational system and the future of our nation. This is the *crystal ball* aspect of the classroom experience.

I assume that a majority of parents have spent some time in their children's classrooms at school. If not, I encourage you to do so. I wish that every American citizen could spend a half-day in a 4th grade, 8th grade, or 11th grade classroom. I believe it is a WYSIWYG experience. In other words, what you see in that classroom will be a good indicator of what our nation is going to experience in the coming years as the students in those classrooms graduate or not, move on to college or not, find suitable careers or not, and begin to run our nation's businesses, government agencies, and other institutions in the best ways they know how. If the classroom experience you see is disjointed and the learning experience is not effective for individual students, ours will become a nation in decline. If you see a coherent classroom experience that is engaging the majority of students in a meaningful learning experience, our nation will continue to lead the world and the American Dream will stay alive and well. This WYSIWYG scenario should cause concern and stimulate interest among all Americans whether you have children or not. Eventually, we will all be living in the future world that today's school children will create. There is much at stake for us all as individuals, families, and communities.

In 2010, NBC News announced its campaign to get Americans involved in becoming an "Education Nation." It is a great concept and a vital commitment that the words "Education Nation" promote. This is a short chapter to encourage all of us to take a greater interest in what goes on in the classrooms of America, whether these classrooms are to be found at your neighborhood schools, online, or at your kitchen table.

Blessings • Challenges

The purpose of education is not to make us "smart" or to give us credentials to brag about. We are already smart. The purpose of education is to expand our awareness of the amazing challenges and opportunities that exist in our world so that we know what we need to do. Then, education provides us with knowledge and skills that further enable us to go do it. —Darby Checketts

SUMMARY
Blessings / Challenges

It is always good to recognize those things in life that are working well. We must forever be reminded to count our blessings. Then, there are those things that are not working so well. These represent our challenges. I would like to share my observations about the public school experience I've been having.

Counting Our Blessings

Here's a list of those things that cause me to be encouraged about the future of our nation and to be thankful for the progress we're making in helping to prepare our children for meaningful and productive lives.

- The majority of the children I see are full of life and willing to learn. Generally, they appear healthy and well cared for. They have cool backpacks and nice shoes. It is likely that their parents or guardians who love them are spending time supporting their educational activities.

- The teachers I meet are amazing. Their dedication is evident. They work tirelessly. They give more back for their salaries received than perhaps any other single group of American professionals.
- Almost all of the classrooms I see are well-organized and decorated in ways that brighten the day, illuminate the learning experience, and remind students of the myriad of principles that make our world go around.
- As a nation, we have made a huge investment in the educational "infrastructure" of buildings, desks, white boards, computers, projectors, lab equipment, cafeteria equipment, and more.
- Increasingly, we use the leverage of computer and internet technology to make learning more individualized and efficient. This technology augments the live instruction that wise and loving teachers provide.
- Finally, *most* of the students I see manage to stay *mostly* on task and to get something of value out of their classroom experiences.

The Challenges

Let me begin this section with reference to the key words "most" and "mostly" that appear in the previous and last sentence of the section above. I believe that "most" and "mostly" are not sufficient. The following observations result from my experiences as both father and substitute teacher. I have given careful consideration as to what might be the specific problems we can address to prevent any sub-optimization of our educational processes. These processes are complex. I cannot point to a list of easy-to-fix problems nor am I in a position to criticize the specific practices of the school teachers and school administrators for whom I have such genuine admiration.

However, there are four related patterns that concern me. I defer to the education experts for a full understanding of what these observations mean and what we can all do about them. Here are my observations based on what I have experienced.

1. The first pattern I notice in nearly every classroom that concerns me most of all is this: There are typically so many students in each class that I wonder how any teacher can find the time to make those personally impactful connections with each child on a regular basis—connections that the teacher surely intends to make that are so important.

2. In many classroom situations, I estimate that there are about 70% (perhaps more) of the students managing to *mostly* stay on task. Another percentage of students are disengaged and some of these are seriously distracted from their learning opportunity.

3. While I know uniform lesson plans are needed to keep a roomful of students all on task at the same time, there are usually a fair number of children whose learning aptitudes don't match a particular lesson plan. For instance, I have personally witnessed the wide range of children's reactions to math. Most students will eventually "get" a particular math concept, but the way their synapses connect around math problems can be so very different. The challenge is to reach more math students in an individualized way. The same challenge exists for reading and other essential skills.

4. There is a basic effort underway to incorporate computers into the public education process. Some school systems are more advanced than others. Some of the computer programs are brilliant and represent a needed change of pace and scenery for students. There are some programs that might

serve mostly to keep students busy or entertained. Computer labs that use desktop or laptop computers with real-time student tracking and computer-guided learning programs appear to provide a more impactful learning experience than does the often less-structured use of individual notepad computers. (I have sometimes found that the small notepad computers are broken or the Wi-Fi doesn't work and these occurrences end up being distractions.)

Quite simply, the biggest challenges we all face are the resource limitations that prevent more individualized instruction. The solutions can only occur as parents become more aware and involved in helping their children to succeed at school, as more teachers and tutors are available to assist students who struggle, and as we give students more access to the highly adaptive learning process that computer-based education can provide so efficiently. What do I recommend?

1. Strengthen American families in every imaginable way. Find more ways to *help parents learn how to help their children learn.* There must be a "culture of learning" in the home.
2. Address student-teacher ratios in any feasible manner.
3. Segment the classroom experience to include more small-group activities and individualized instruction for those students who need it most.
4. Continue the national conversation around computer-based education to make it more accessible and to provide support for those technology solutions that have the greatest merit. With the significant challenges we face, educators and parents must reinvent themselves around computer and Internet technology.

Everything we cherish as Americans is at stake: our economic prosperity, our national security, and our leadership role in the world. We must make learning more individually supportive of and responsive to each and every child. This is a huge goal because there are so many children, too few teachers, and so much to learn in this complex world of the 21st Century.

Let me conclude with a word about higher education. The focus of the church and community service work that Sharon and I have been doing is to support current and prospective college students. We are inspired by the spirit and intent of Utah's "Prosperity 2020" initiative and other visionary commitments to the future of our great state and our nation. Our purpose is to help high school and college students become more interested in, ready for, and likely to succeed at higher education. Our goals are for each student to…

1. Make the connection between "educational attainment" and family financial security, professional fulfillment, personal goal achievement, and the many opportunities for community service and leadership,
2. Recognize the golden opportunity that is theirs as the economy grows and there is an expanding need for well-educated and technologically-skilled (STEM) workers to fill the exciting jobs of the future,
3. Set clear goals for college completion and lifelong learning.

Those of us who now live in the Great State of Utah acknowledge the vision of the early pioneers who settled our valleys and established our fine communities. Among their most profound legacies is Utah's collection of outstanding colleges and universities. We are blessed to have access to such high quality yet affordable education. As Utahns, we must be exemplary in how we conduct the education of our children, our youth, and the adults who make learning a lifelong pursuit.

Darby Checketts

The book is my way to honor school teachers. It is my attempt to help lift the educational horizons of students and their parents. It is my message to my fellow Americans about the all-importance of education.

THE AUTHOR
My Life in the Classroom

As did most Americans, I spent nearly half of the waking hours during my childhood and young adulthood in a classroom. Usually, this classroom was at school. Sometimes, the classroom was at the kitchen table at my mother's elbow. There was my "Sunday School" classroom. And, there was that special classroom that encircled the campfire where my Scoutmaster would teach us to love the outdoors, to respect each other, and to practice the skills of personal preparedness.

I was blessed to have mostly gifted and loving teachers who imparted valuable knowledge to me and who helped me to build my sense of self-worth. For the most part, I loved my teachers. A few seemed too stern or too academic. And, there were just a few who put me to sleep.

Throughout my life, I have held a deep respect for school teachers. I appreciated their commitment to me as a young person. As I grew older, I began to realize the sacrifices good teachers make to benefit our communities and our nation.

I thought I might like to become a teacher, but too many people told me that teachers were overworked and underpaid. Not that I was lazy and avaricious, but I simply wanted the financial leverage that I figured the business world might offer instead.

Of the many college courses I took, those in the social sciences intrigued me most. As I explored the possibilities for a purposeful career in the business world, I began to respond to these ideas: leadership, teamwork, customer service, and overall organizational effectiveness. I knew there was a vital "people" side to every business and I could earn a good living while helping employees experience a more meaningful and productive work life as they served their customers well.

Upon my graduation from Brigham Young University, I was hired by Ford Motor Company in Dearborn, Michigan. My initial assignment was at the Lincoln-Mercury Division in the "Salary Administration" section of what would be known today as the HR or Human Resources department.

I soon tired of the salary administration duties. A friend of mine told me of a "Training Specialist" position at the Ford Design Center. I applied and got the job. It was this job that would define me professionally and shape the next half-century of my life, and cause me to spend thousands of days in the classroom.

At the Design Center, my initial assignments were to update the HR guidelines for Design Center supervisors and then to explain these in small group training sessions. I enjoyed making presentations and interacting with groups. These experiences revealed the aptitudes I had earlier demonstrated in high school as I participated in student government and various community service projects.

I was on my way to becoming an "educator" within the business world. I vividly remember one tipping point. I was approached by the Design Center HR manager who had a special assignment in mind. He said, "Darby, I've noticed that you are a particularly good explainer of things. You know how to energize people to new ways of thinking. We are about to introduce a new program throughout the Design Center called MBO, which stands for 'Management by Objectives.' We would like to have you develop a full-day training workshop and to teach it to all of our managers and supervisors during the coming months." I had found my calling. As the years have gone by, I have developed dozens of workshops and I have presented these to over 300 organizations in 27 countries around the world with audiences totaling in the hundreds of thousands.

I have worked for five corporations as a trainer or as an internal consultant for organizational effectiveness. In 1985, I established my own consulting firm, Cornerstone Professional Development. For more than a quarter-century, I lived the life of the so-called "road warrior." I traveled and I taught. As my repertoire of useful ideas and practical methods began to accumulate, I undertook the role of author.

During my very interesting and colorful career as a traveling trainer, I kept my home ties strong and always understood that all the teaching I might do across the world would not amount to much of an accomplishment if my own children were not well taught at home and at school. They were blessed to have a most conscientious mother. Her college degree is in Elementary Education with an emphasis on "Child Development and Family Relations." She kept that kitchen table classroom humming just as my own mother had done. Our children have been further blessed to have school teachers who challenged and inspired them. Each of our children has gone on to obtain one or more college degrees.

As I have grown older and watched my children mature, I have more and more realized how much I owe to their dedicated school teachers. At the same time, I recognize that the family is the foundation of society and the most important learning occurs there. School teachers usually augment the positive things that occur in the home as each child develops. Conversely, many school teachers must compensate for failures in the home. If parents don't manage to reach through to their children, it may be that a school teacher is a child's best hope for those breakthroughs in self-concept and learning that will help her or him to achieve success and happiness in life.

In 2007, a great economic recession came upon America. Our family-owned consulting business continued to go forward though I knew a time would come when, like that veteran Texas Ranger, I would hang my *PowerPoint* holster on the wall and settle down. I contemplated the opportunity to spend more time enjoying our posterity that, as of this moment, includes 34 grandchildren. I had more books to write and many places to which I intended to travel with Sharon.

I began to look for creative ways to fill those "in-between" days that would become available to me. Sharon and I received an assignment within the Church of Jesus Christ of Latter-day Saints to participate in the LDS Inner City Project. We serve as Education Specialists supporting the Hispanic congregations in the Salt Lake City area. During the past several years, we have been privileged to work with more than 400 bright and delightful students.

As I considered various "semi-retirement" activities, I decided that it might be fun to turn back the clock and become that public school teacher I had once considered becoming. I chose to apply for a substitute teacher position within the Jordan School District. I was accepted. I have been substituting for much of the current school year. It has been a most enjoyable and enlightening experience. The inspiration for this book has come about naturally and without premeditation. The book is my way to honor school teachers. It is my attempt to help lift the educational horizons of students and their parents. It is my message to my fellow Americans about the all-importance of education. As we've often heard from NBC News, we must become an *Education Nation*.

As a substitute teacher, I have taught students in grades 1, 2, 3, 4, 5, 6, 7, 8, 9, 10, 11, and 12. Some of these assignments have been to serve primarily as the classroom ringmaster. Most have involved the execution of excellent lesson plans with honest-to-goodness opportunities to teach. I can tell you this, whatever the backgrounds of substitute teachers happen to be, there are important disciplines we "subs" must possess. A substitute has to (a) assimilate a great deal of information in a very short amount of time, (b) think quickly on his/her feet, and (c) be a competent communicator and friendly disciplinarian at the same time.

I have learned so much from the three great CLASSROOM experiences of my life…

1. Initially, *I sat in the classroom* at the feet of elementary, high school, and college instructors.
2. Then, *I stood at the front of the classroom* for over four decades as I worked to expand the vision and lift the horizons of employees in over 300 client organizations.

3. And, now comes my third great opportunity *to stand before* the most important audience of all—those precious children and young adults who will lead American society into the 21st Century. As we face daunting challenges as a nation, we will be no smarter at solving our problems than our educational programs are preparing our children to be.

As I walk into each new classroom and begin to interact with the students, I get impressions about what seems to be working well or not. I rejoice in the programs and lesson plans that are creative and powerful. At the same time, my years of teaching experience help me to recognize when something is lacking. I see children who are engaged. I see children who are holding back or who are too distracted to learn much. I experience the overwhelming sense of responsibility that dedicated school teachers must feel every day that inspires them to carry on. Building on (or overcoming) what happens in each child's home, the teacher in the classroom is often key to those physical, emotional, intellectual, and spiritual breakthroughs that will play a major role in shaping each child's potential for success and happiness. Aside from the loving influence of good parents, there is no more important responsibility in our society than that of school teacher.

Finally, as a substitute teacher, let me conclude with this. I have traveled to faraway places and have become involved with "great" causes, but there is no more powerful moment than when I look into the eager faces of a roomful of fourth graders and have one of them come to me with a so-serious concern that requires my simplest yet most profound reassurance. Suddenly, life's priorities are crystal clear for me.

Please visit our "Education / Classroom" website at:
www.prep4ed.com

For further information, please contact:
Cornerstone Pro-Dev Press
P. O. Box 95961
South Jordan, UT 84095
Telephone: 801-253-0895 or 866-654-0811
Email: info@prep4ed.com

This book and Darby Checketts' many other books are available at Amazon.com and through all other book retailers. The most recent and popular titles include:

Leverage: How to Create Your Own "Tipping Points"
Customer Astonishment: 10 Secrets to World-Class Customer Care
The New American Prosperity
You Can Bet Your Life on God
Positive Conflict: Transform Opposition into Innovation
Who Owns the World? – The Parable of Tehya

Notes

Made in the USA
Charleston, SC
17 September 2013